He needed to get to the big bin van to be emptied but nobody could move him.

"I could then be recycled to make a shiny new bottle."

From the bottle bank I would be taken to the glass treatment plant.

There I would be sorted by colour and washed to remove any impurities.

Then I would be crushed and melted...

...before being moulded into a brand new bottle.

"That would be much better than sitting at the bottom of a landfill site and spoiling the countryside."

"And we could be delivering next week's news, if we were recycled," chorused an army of newspapers and magazines, as they struggled to get out of Bertie.

Taylor climbed out of Bertie and set off in search of a new owner.

First he had a wash so that he was nice and clean.

Then he waited to be picked up by a charity collection van.

And in no time at all he was on display in a charity shop...

... where he was bought by somebody new.

I look great! I'm certainly not ready for the bin yet!

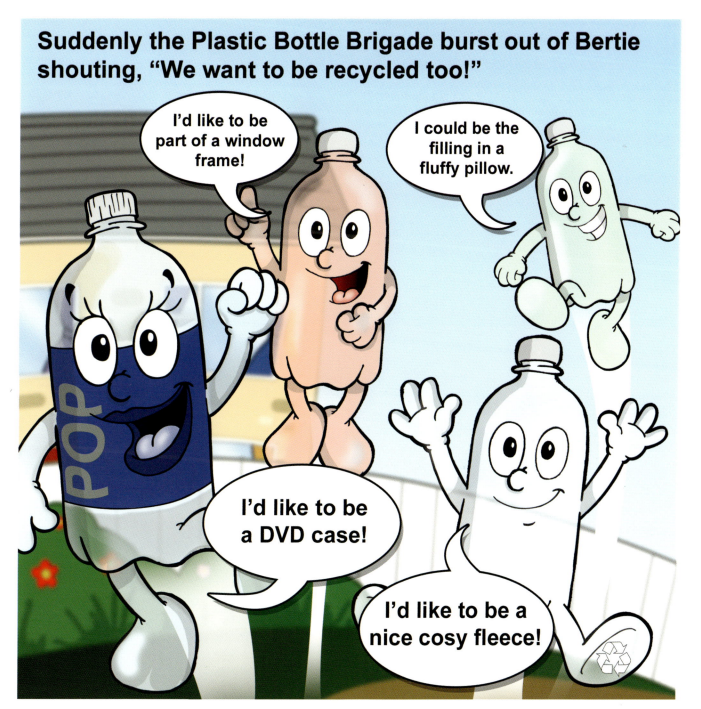

And following the bottles came the vegetable peelings in search of a compost heap.

"We can rot down to make lovely compost that will help new plants to grow," said Curly Carrot Top.

Bertie was very happy. With so many things that could be recycled he need never feel so full again.

He was wheeled to the big bin van for the last little bits of rubbish to be emptied.

Exit Ramp Underworld

Written by Marianne Posadas
Illustrated by Linhan Ye

Contents

1	In the Darkness	4
2	Do Not Disturb	8
3	Let Me Be at Peace	15
4	A Horrifying Discovery	21
5	A Frightening Day	29
6	Something Weird	37
7	A Ghoul Revealed	45

Meet the Characters

Adriana Allman

One of the Allman twins.

Annabelle Allman

The other Allman twin.

Mr Corbett

A Department of Roads worker.

Mr Gregory

Another Department of Roads worker.

Jebediah Allman and friends

The inhabitants of the old Ingleford cemetery.

A Crow

The guardian of the old Ingleford cemetery.

Dear Reader

Many years ago, in my home town, a new road was built through an old cemetery. I thought it must have been spooky working there, and I'm sure not everyone agreed with the plans to disturb the old tombs and gravestones. That event gave me the idea for this horror story. I hope you enjoy it - but be warned - don't read it alone!

Marianne Posadas
Author

Ingleford Cemetery

1. Ingleford School
2. The old Ingleford cemetery
3. The Allman house
4. Ingleford main street

1 In the Darkness

The torch flickered ominously. The life in its tiny bulb petered into nothing. Suddenly, the room was plunged into an eerie darkness. The shadowy walls seemed to be closing in.

No one breathed. Slowly, as her eyes became accustomed to the gloom, Adriana Allman put down the book of horror stories from which she'd been reading aloud. She jumped in alarm when she saw the shape of her twin sister's head hovering in front of her.

"Annabelle!" she hissed. "Annabelle, don't move!"

The moon slipped out from behind a cloud. Annabelle's head became connected to a neck, shoulders and torso. Despite Adriana's plea, Annabelle's dark form loomed over her sister. Her eyes widened.

"Don't come any closer," hissed Adriana, with a growing sense of foreboding.

Then something clattered noisily to the ground. Annabelle's ghostly outline stumbled and let out a cry. Adriana clamped her eyes shut, her worst fears confirmed. Urgently, her fingers scrabbled on the wall next to her.

Where was it? Where? Where? Adriana searched in vain. Then, as she was about to leap out of bed and fling open the door, her fingers bumped into something. An enormous feeling of relief swept over her.

She flicked on the light switch. The dark room was transformed in an instant. The Allman twins recoiled involuntarily and blinked.

Adriana looked at the red stain slowly spreading across the floor. Her fingers reached out to touch the sticky dampness.

Annabelle looked at the scene in horror. Adriana's eyes, filled with anxiety, flicked upwards at her sister.

Annabelle crept downstairs, step by step, holding her breath with each footfall. The still night air seemed to magnify every creak emanating from the protesting floorboards. She glanced over her shoulder. No one else in the house stirred.

Silently, she felt her way towards the laundry. There, salvation in the form of a bucket and a sponge awaited. If she could blot out the evidence before the morning, no one would ever know.

In the darkness, Annabelle's fingers passed over the cupboards until they fell upon the handle she wanted. Without a sound, she grasped the handle. Slowly, she opened the cupboard.

With an almighty clatter, an army of demented brooms, mops, buckets and dustpans fell on her!

Worse still, as she scrambled backwards, she heard the sound she had been most dreading. A single heavy footstep coming from the other bedroom.

Annabelle's heart plunged. There was nothing for it. She was about to meet her fate!

2 Do Not Disturb

"I told you not to move," said Adriana. "I told you."

"How was I meant to know where you'd left your raspberry cordial?" said Annabelle, looking downcast. "I was only trying to find the light switch."

Teresa, the twins' mother, shook her head. She looked at the spilled raspberry cordial soaking into the carpet.

"You girls!" she said in exasperation. "How many times have I told you not to read by torchlight? It's bad for your eyes – and the carpet."

"Sorry, Mum," said the twins in unison.

"I'll clean it up," added Annabelle.

"*The Grim Graveyard of Ghastly Ghouls*," said Teresa, reading the title of Adriana's book. "Whatever next?"

"*The Shadowy Sepulchre of Silent Shame!*" piped up Adriana. "It's a whole series from our school book club and ..."

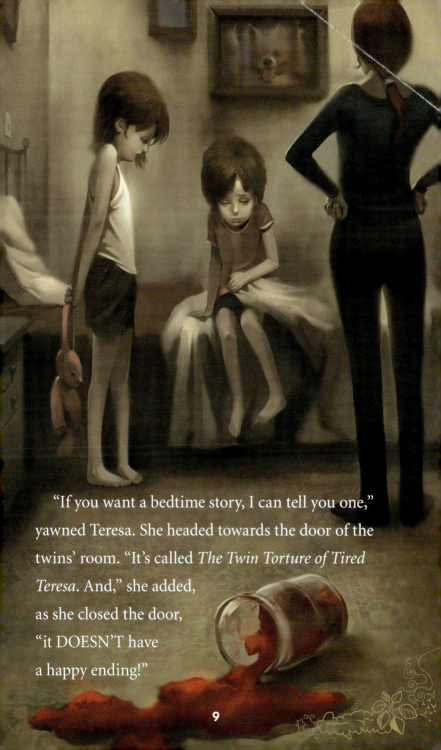

"If you want a bedtime story, I can tell you one," yawned Teresa. She headed towards the door of the twins' room. "It's called *The Twin Torture of Tired Teresa*. And," she added, as she closed the door, "it DOESN'T have a happy ending!"

The next morning, the sound of the toaster popping made the twins jump. They were still tired after their midnight adventures.

Hidden behind the pages of the *Ingleford Crier*, the town's morning newspaper, Ralph, the twins' father, was grumbling about politicians, police officers, protesters and pretty much everyone else. He liked talking to the newspaper – and the morning radio reports and the evening TV news.

The twins had noticed their father getting grumpier and grumpier as time passed. Years ago, he'd worked as a special effects supervisor on movies and television shows, but with the rise of computer-generated effects, the demand for real explosions, remote-controlled car chases and spectacular effects had dried up. Now, instead of remote-controlled car chases, he worked installing remote-controlled garage doors. The highlight of his year was being in charge of Ingleford's New Year's Eve fireworks display, but a rainy night had made sure that even that had been a fizzer this year.

Teresa juggled the hot toast and dropped a slice on everyone's plate. Adriana and Annabelle were relieved that the terrible tale of the tortured twins had not come to anything. In fact, the greatest horror of the new day had been the discovery that they'd run out of peanut butter.

"WHAT?" bellowed the twins' father suddenly.

The twins jumped like two freshly toasted slices of bread leaping out of the toaster.

Ralph's face appeared from behind the drooping newspaper wearing an expression that looked like he'd just swallowed a hornet. He peered at the article  in front of him in disbelief and then stared at Teresa, Adriana and Annabelle.

"What's the matter, Dad?" asked Annabelle.

Ralph took a sip of his steaming coffee and jabbed his finger at the offending newspaper story.

"They've finally given the go-ahead for our town's new freeway off-ramp," he said.

Ralph furiously gulped another mouthful of hot coffee.

"That's good, isn't it?" said Mum with a puzzled look. "An off-ramp will make it easier to get in and out of town. More cars. More garage doors," she added hopefully.

"Yes, yes, yes," spluttered Ralph. "But look where it's going! They're going to dig up the old Ingleford cemetery and put the off-ramp right through the middle of it!"

"Surely not," said Teresa.

Ralph handed over the newspaper.

"'The old Ingleford cemetery has not been used for over a century,'" read Teresa. "'The town council has granted the Department of Roads a permit to use the land as long as they move the headstones somewhere safe. Mr Corbett, an official with the department, said that they would start work soon.'"

"I can't believe it," said Ralph. "I know it's been over a hundred years since the cemetery was used, but even so ..."

"It's kind of spooky in there," said Annabelle. "We sometimes walk home from school through the old cemetery. Nobody uses it."

Ralph fixed his daughter with a stare he usually kept for TV newsreaders or people who wrote letters to the newspaper editor.

"Your great-great-grandfather is using it," he said. "He's been using it since 1918 and he probably doesn't want to be disturbed."

Annabelle looked at her toast awkwardly. She had forgotten about the mossy, overgrown headstone that marked the spot where Jebediah, the town's first Allman, had been buried three generations ago.

"Well, if they're going to move the headstones somewhere, at least we can go and visit Jebediah without having to push our way through thorn bushes and waist-high thistles," said Teresa. "It is a little unkempt."

"That's not the point," said Ralph, hiding behind the paper again. "It's a historic place and it shouldn't be disturbed."

The remainder of breakfast was filled with harrumphs and snorts and words like "rubbish", "nonsense" and "vandals".

The rest of the family ate their toast in silence. But, for once, Annabelle, Adriana and Teresa agreed with the conversation Ralph was having with the paper. A freeway off-ramp through the old Ingleford cemetery didn't seem right.

3 Let Me Be at Peace

Mr Corbett pushed the bright yellow Department of Roads hard hat onto his head, adjusted his glasses, and opened the door of the ute.

A tangled boxthorn scratched noisily over the door panel and Mr Corbett found himself wedged between the ute and a mass of twigs and prickles.

He gingerly squeezed around the back of the ute. Despite his efforts, he emerged covered in dry dust and old cobwebs, a dozen twigs and thorns embedded in his overalls.

His companion, Mr Gregory, was already surveying the tombs, vaults and headstones throughout the old cemetery.

"Clearing all this up won't take a bulldozer more than a couple of days," he said, waving his arm across the vista of scrub, weeds and cracked concrete paving jutting up at crazy angles.

A thin, dusty path, used by the local schoolchildren as a shortcut, wove its way through the scrub. A single black crow, perched on a lichen-covered stone angel, gazed at them suspiciously.

"The tombs and vaults are all cracked. Their foundations are sinking. They'll be easy to demolish. It's removing all the headstones that will take the time," agreed Mr Corbett. He read an inscription on a nearby stone. "Jezebel Limmer, born 1834, died 1886. She will not be forgotten."

Mr Gregory raised an eyebrow. "By the looks of this place, she's been well and truly forgotten," he observed. "These thistles are more like trees than weeds!"

Under the eye of the lone black crow, the two men pushed their way through the undergrowth, stopping here and there to read another headstone or to shake the iron gates to the tombs. They began to measure up the old cemetery, but it was impossible to lay out tapes or mark spots with chalk.

Absorbed in their task, and trying not to twist their ankles in hidden rabbit holes, Mr Corbett and Mr Gregory's attention was firmly fixed on the uneven ground beneath their feet.

They did not notice the drop in temperature, as a chilly breeze hurried in from the northwest, nor the morning sun retreating slowly behind the grey clouds gathering over Ingleford.

"This is hopeless," said Mr Corbett. For the third time, his tape had become snagged in the weeds. "We'll have to clear all this away before we even start drawing up a plan for the off-ramp."

He stood up and turned impatiently. Suddenly, the gallery of clouds that had been circling the area burst into life.

A huge roll of thunder echoed through the air, and the lone crow took flight with a frightened *craw-craw*. Mr Corbett looked up in alarm, and turned towards the ute.

Mr Gregory was already there, waving urgently. Mr Corbett tried to take a step forward, but he found his right foot was firmly rooted to the ground, as if a ghoulish hand had clasped it tight.

"Aargh!" cried Mr Corbett, as he felt himself topple. He flung his arms out wildly and closed his eyes. A split-second later, his hard-hat cracked on the concrete base of a hidden headstone and his body thumped onto the ground.

Mr Corbett groaned and opened his eyes. Another peal of thunder split the sky and large raindrops started pelting down. He blinked. Directly in front of him was an inscription. As the rain dribbled into the letters carved in stone, the old words seemed to shout at Mr Corbett.

"From this final hour, Let me be at peace, FOREVER."

Mr Corbett twisted his body and saw that his foot was wedged under a hawthorn root. He struggled to release it. When he finally pulled himself free, he clambered to his feet.

"Are you OK?" called Mr Gregory.

"I'll be fine," replied Mr Corbett, rubbing his elbows. He put the weight of his frame onto the freed foot and was relieved to find it wasn't broken.

He collected his tape and hard-hat and pushed his way through wet thistles and thorn bushes to the path.

Inside the cabin of the ute, he looked at Mr Gregory. Mr Corbett was shivering, but he wasn't sure if it was the cold raindrops creeping down his neck or something else.

"We're going to have to mark out all the safety hazards in this place," Mr Corbett said. "We'll have to tell them this will take a few more days than we expected."

In the background came the faint *craw-craw* of a solitary crow.

4   A Horrifying Discovery

The attic of the Allman house was dark and musty. The dusty remnants of a century's worth of spider webs lay draped in the corners.

"They're up here somewhere," coughed Adriana, as she opened yet another dust-covered box. "Mum and Dad never throw anything out. They would have stored them up here with all the other old bits and pieces last time we cleared the bedroom out."

After last night's accident, Annabelle and Adriana had decided to retrieve the old bedside lamps which, when they were younger, had been in their bedroom. Reading midnight horror stories by lamplight instead of torchlight wouldn't be quite so atmospheric, but would probably avoid any further raspberry cordial mishaps.

The attic, which was like a hidden graveyard for old furniture, boxes and suitcases, was accessed through a single trapdoor. When the twins had first clambered up the attic ladder, there had been enough light coming through the trapdoor to see clearly. But now, with the sudden rainstorm clattering on the roof, the attic was filled with dark shadows.

"Old photo albums," said Annabelle, tucking in the edges of a box she'd just pulled open. "What's in there?"

Adriana examined the box in front of her. "Old books," she said, drawing out an old, well-thumbed paperback novel. She pushed the box towards the back of the pile, and opened another. She tried to make out the dim shape inside the box. Then, with a dawning feeling of horror, she drew back in fright.

"Aargh!" she screamed.

"What is it?" said Annabelle in alarm. "What's in the box?" She raced over to her sister, whose eyes were like pale saucers in the gloom.

"It's ... it's ..." stammered Adriana.

Trembling, Annabelle mustered up the courage to look inside the shadowy cardboard box.

Then she reeled backwards. There, staring at her sightlessly, were two bloodshot eyes, sunk deeply in a shrivelled head, severed at the neck!

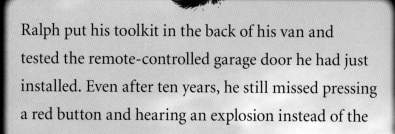

Ralph put his toolkit in the back of his van and tested the remote-controlled garage door he had just installed. Even after ten years, he still missed pressing a red button and hearing an explosion instead of the whirr of a gliding door.

His mind had been on other things all morning, but he was relieved to see that the new door worked.

"Here's your remote, Mrs Hitchcock," he said to the garage owner, who'd come out to check progress.

"You seem a little distracted today, Ralph," said Mrs Hitchcock, pocketing the remote control. "Is everything OK?"

"I've been thinking about the off-ramp they're going to put through the old cemetery," replied Ralph. "It's just not right."

"I saw that in the paper," said Mrs Hitchcock, shaking her head. "My great-uncle is there, you know. Along with many of the founders of our town."

Ralph shut the door of his van and put his hands in his pockets.

"Someone should do something," he said.

"Someone should," agreed Mrs Hitchcock. In her pocket, her fingers found the red button in the middle of the remote and she pressed it.

Ralph, who had been thinking of tombs and vaults and headstones, jumped at the sudden noise of the garage door bursting into life.

"Crikey, Mrs Hitchcock. You almost scared the living daylights out of me with that thing," he grinned.

Mrs Hitchcock smiled. "Sorry," she said. "It's just exciting to have a door that seems to open by itself. Quite spooky, really."

"Hmm," said Ralph. A tiny idea was flickering in the deepest depths of his mind. "I suppose it is, isn't it?"

He climbed into the driver's seat of his van.

"Have a nice day, Mrs Hitchcock," said Ralph. He clicked his seatbelt, looked over his shoulder and reversed slowly down the driveway.

Finding a severed, bloody head in their attic was the last thing that the Allman twins had expected.

"We should call the police," hissed Adriana.

"No, Adriana, we can't do that," quavered Annabelle.

"Why not?" asked her sister.

"Adriana, who do you think put that box up here?" said Annabelle. "It must have been either Mum or Dad!"

Adriana was dumbstruck. Her sister was right. The awful realisation of what that meant slowly dawned on her. She stared at her twin sister.

After a minute's excruciating silence, Adriana spoke softly. "Who do you think the head belongs to?" she said.

Annabelle shook her head. "I don't know. I didn't get a good look."

"Go and see if you recognise the face," said Adriana.

"No way!" burst out Annabelle fiercely. "You go and look."

"You saw it first," insisted Adriana.

Another minute of silent dread passed. Then Annabelle stood up reluctantly and slowly edged closer to the box. She grimaced and closed her eyes. Then, hoping that Adriana couldn't see her shaking in the gloom, she forced herself to look inside.

The bloodied head stared back at her accusingly.

Against all her instincts, Annabelle tried to focus on the sunken, lifeless face. "Something's not quite right about it," she whispered to Adriana.

"Discovering a severed head in the attic is definitely not quite right," agreed Adriana vehemently.

"No, I mean the eyes and the mouth," said Annabelle, drawing a little closer to the gory object. "They don't quite look human."

Adriana was astonished to see her sister reach out a fearful hand. She couldn't believe it. "You're not going to touch it?" she breathed in horror. "Don't do it!"

But Annabelle's hand disappeared into the box. Her fingers touched the head for a split-second and she flinched. In that instant, her bravery melted away. The horror of discovering that at least one of her parents was a bloodthirsty murderer was too much for her thumping heart and spinning head.

"Let's get out of here," she wailed. Adriana was already halfway down the ladder out of the attic.

5 A Frightening Day

Mr Corbett and Mr Gregory had their meeting with the Department of Roads. It had been agreed that they should spend the rest of the week marking out the dangers and pitfalls of the Ingleford cemetery site before any demolition work began.

The crosses and circles that Mr Corbett and Mr Gregory needed to spray on the tombs and undergrowth would require a lot of aerosol cans filled with fluorescent-red paint. The next morning, they headed downstairs to the supply warehouse and filled out the forms they needed.

A store assistant came back with a carton full of spray cans.

"With this much fluorescent paint, the entire site will glow at night," he joked.

"You wouldn't catch me in there at night," muttered Mr Corbett. He rubbed his elbow, still sore from his morning tumble. "That place gives me the creeps, even during daylight."

"You aren't scared by old graveyards, are you?" laughed Mr Gregory.

"Of course not," snorted Mr Corbett unenthusiastically. "I just don't want my ankle broken next time." He looked at Mr Gregory, feeling a little unconvinced. He was as level-headed as the next man – but if Mr Gregory didn't feel just a tiny bit uneasy about working in a place surrounded by tombs, vaults and headstones, he was the only one.

A feeling of unease was exactly what the Allman twins were sharing – magnified a thousandfold. They'd agreed to say nothing about their ghastly discovery but, to them, the silence around the breakfast table the next morning was deafening.

The toast popped out of the toaster, shattering the stillness and making the girls leap out of their skins. Ralph straightened his newspaper and Teresa spread butter over her toast, the blade of her butter knife glinting evilly in the morning light. On the surface, everything was normal – but behind the facade of normality, everything had changed. The twins had an awful, simultaneous thought. How long would it be before one – or both – of their parents was featured on the front page of the *Ingleford Crier*? For all the wrong reasons.

"'Surveying to continue,'" boomed Ralph suddenly, reading from the paper. "'The Department of Roads will push forward with its plans once a health-and-safety survey of the old town cemetery is completed.'"

His eyes appeared above the edge of the newspaper.

There was a dark look in their father's eyes that the twins had never noticed before.

"Really?" he growled, as he disappeared behind the newsprint once more. He let out a deep chuckle that chilled Annabelle and Adriana to the bone.

Annabelle and Adriana headed towards their school. The morning was overcast and drizzly, so they took the shortcut through the old cemetery.

"We have to do something about that head," said Adriana, dragging herself reluctantly along the path.

"I know," said Annabelle, shuddering. "After school, we need to go up into the attic again and get that box."

Suddenly, there was a rustle in the undergrowth, followed by a low hissing noise.

A single black crow flew into the air, swooping low above their heads.

"What was that?" said Annabelle, clutching her sister's arm in alarm.

Adriana whirled around towards the source of the sound. Everything fell silent.

"I heard something," hissed Annabelle. "Did you?"

Adriana nodded grimly. The twins stood like statues in the middle of the path, straining their ears for another sound.

There was nothing except the sound of the morning drizzle. Then, suddenly, there it was! Something in the tangled undergrowth to their left hissed again.

Adriana picked up a stone from the edge of a puddle on the path.

"It's probably just another crow," she said warily. "This should scare it away."

She aimed the stone at the spot where the noise was coming from and threw it as hard as she could.

"Ouch!" came a startled cry from the undergrowth. The twins stumbled backwards. A bright-yellow hard-hat emerged from the bushes. Beneath it, a furious face was glaring towards them.

"Clear out!" called the face. The figure waved an angry arm at the girls. At the end of the arm, they saw a hand, ominously splattered with something glowing deep red.

"It's blood!" yelled Adriana in a panic.

The figure took a step towards them. The girls suddenly found their feet and sprinted along the path towards the schoolyard on the other side of the cemetery.

Finally, they reached safety. Panting, they forced themselves to look back towards the figure with the bloodied hand. There was nothing there. The figure had disappeared.

"What is going on?" cried Annabelle.

One day ago, the twins' life had been entirely normal. Now, they'd been unwillingly thrust into a real-life horror movie.

The school day passed in a slow, agonising blur. The other schoolchildren seemed blissfully unaware of the terrible events unfolding around them. Neither Annabelle nor Adriana could concentrate on anything. They sat silently, feeling like an enormous burden was weighing down on them.

After six interminable hours, the bell for hometime rang. And when the twins finally arrived home – avoiding the shortcut – and climbed up the ladder to the attic, another horrifying discovery awaited.

"It's gone," gasped Adriana, staring at her sister in alarm. "The severed head is gone!"

A chill of foreboding crept down the twins' spines and beads of sweat broke out on their foreheads. They both knew what that meant. Someone had been up in the attic. And someone would know that the box had been disturbed. It was only a matter of time before that someone realised who had disturbed it.

6 Something Weird

Ralph finished his handiwork, allowing himself a satisfied smile. He rested against the grey headstone sheltering him from the afternoon drizzle.

"That's the evidence taken care of, Jebediah," he said under his breath. "No one will suspect a thing." He'd taken care to not be observed, completing his task slowly and carefully. He allowed himself a moment's rest. Then he glanced at the cardboard box that lay at his feet. He reached down and pulled out its cold, rubbery contents.

Mr Corbett pushed his way out of the bushes and strode out of the cemetery. He looked around for Mr Gregory. He was wet, cold and covered in mud.

"How long does it take to get another carton of spray paint?" he muttered. "I sent Gregory off hours ago to replenish our supply."

Mr Corbett looked at his watch in irritation. He was about to call Mr Gregory on his mobile phone when he heard a reassuring crunching of tyres on gravel. The Department of Roads ute pulled up in front of him.

"Sorry," said Mr Gregory. "They'd run out of red paint. We have to use fluorescent green instead."

"Well, that's better than nothing," said Mr Corbett. He grabbed a can and tossed another one to Mr Gregory. "Come on. There are still plenty of hazards to spray-paint."

The pair of men followed the pathway into the cemetery – but after about twenty metres, they stopped.

"What was that?" asked Mr Corbett with a puzzled look on his face. "I'm sure I heard something coming from over by that tomb."

Mr Gregory looked over at the crumbling structure, with an iron gate sagging across its entrance. Like a constant foreboding omen, the cemetery crow sat accusingly on the flat roof.

"Sounded like something creaking and squealing," he said in surprise.

Then, both men's jaws dropped.

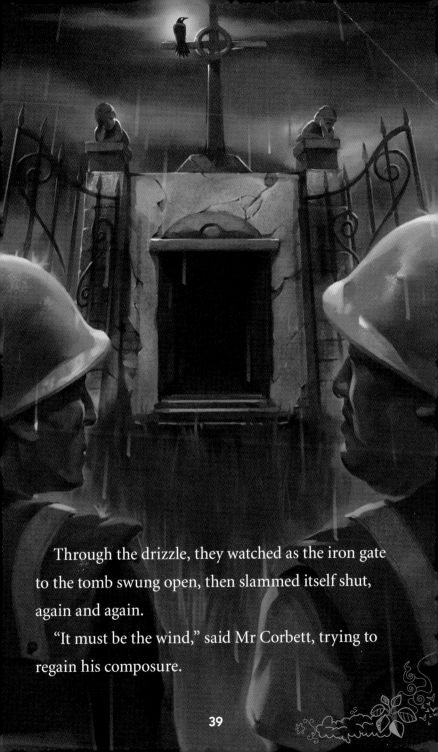

Through the drizzle, they watched as the iron gate to the tomb swung open, then slammed itself shut, again and again.

"It must be the wind," said Mr Corbett, trying to regain his composure.

"I hate to tell you this," said Mr Gregory, "but there isn't any wind."

The gate ceased its eerie clanking and the two men took a few paces forward. Suddenly, they were riveted to the spot once more.

"Over there!" exclaimed Mr Corbett. "This time, it's that old marble tomb."

Both men stared in horror at the marble tomb, its gate opening and shutting as if it were waving at them, beckoning them to come closer, closer!

"I don't like this," said Mr Corbett. "Something weird is going on."

The twins sat in their room. Annabelle had a nagging thought.

"Do you think there's any connection between the mysterious figure with the blood-soaked hand and the missing head?" she finally blurted. "Surely it can't be a coincidence that there are suddenly two scary mysteries in this small town?"

"Maybe," mused Adriana. "The figure didn't seem too happy to see us."

"Let's go back and see what it was up to," said Annabelle decisively. "Surely it can't still be there. We have to find out what's going on. Then we're going straight to the police."

Reluctantly, Adriana agreed and the twins pulled on their raincoats.

Mr Corbett and Mr Gregory knew they had to carry on. There had to be some logical explanation for the strange tomb gates opening and shutting wildly in the still air. The men pushed their way into the undergrowth and pulled the caps off their spray cans.

"Spray here," directed Mr Corbett. "We need to mark this out. There's a huge rabbit warren here."

Suddenly, there was a clamour of iron gates, all squealing and clanging in protest. The terrified men looked at each other.

In the next instant, the dreary grey cemetery was lit up with a flash. Then another. And another. Smoke rose from three corners. All the while, the deathly clanging of the gates continued, like a rusty, ghastly chorus.

"I've had enough," declared Mr Corbett, whose nerves had finally come to the end of their tether.

"Me too," said Mr Gregory, who was at a loss to explain the mysterious goings-on.

Both men turned around and leapt in fright. Amidst the flashing and clanging, a figure had crept up behind them, unseen and unheard. And when the men saw its ghoulish face and the rivulets of blood dripping from its neck, they screamed. Mr Corbett accidentally let off a burst of fluorescent-green paint from the spray can he was gripping tightly in his hand.

Then the two men ran for their lives.

"There's nothing here," said Annabelle, her hair wet and dripping from the drizzle. She pushed back the bushes. "But it looks like someone's been spray-painting the ground. Why would they do that?"

Adriana huddled beside her, shivering in the drizzle. "Maybe they're marking the spot where something is buried," she said.

The twins looked at each other. They both knew what Adriana was referring to.

"I've seen all I want to see," said Annabelle. "I'm going to the police station. Are you coming?"

"I'm not staying out here," said Adriana grimly. "And I'm definitely not going home alone."

The twins turned. And froze. Nothing could have prepared them for the sight in front of them.

"Hello, Adriana. Hello, Annabelle."

**IT WAS THE MISSING SEVERED HEAD.
IT WAS GLOWING FLUORESCENT GREEN.
IT WAS ATTACHED TO A BODY.
AND IT KNEW THEIR NAMES!**

7 A Ghoul Revealed

The severed head let out a chuckle and its sunken bloodshot eyes fixed the twins with a cold, unblinking stare.

Annabelle and Adriana stood transfixed, their blood running cold.

Then, to their amazement, the figure reached up, grasped the bloody wound across its neck and pulled.

The cold, rubbery skin peeled off. And there stood the twins' father, grinning sheepishly.

"Sorry," he said. "I forgot I still had that on."

The twins stared at Ralph. They were speechless.

In the darkness of the attic, the twins and their father pushed heavy cardboard boxes back into place.

"It's an old special-effects mask," Ralph had explained. "Looks pretty realistic, huh? I was good back in my heyday."

He emptied the bag of spare remote-control garage door openers into another box.

"Better keep these away from prying eyes, too," he winked. "People might be tempted to use them for all sorts of things besides garage doors."

At first the twins had been ready to burst into tears. Then they had been furious. Then they had been astounded. Finally, when their father swore them to secrecy and persuaded them to help him put his old special-effects gear back into the attic, they grew secretly impressed. Who would have thought that Ralph Allman, garage door installer, would have dreamed up such a scenario?

"All I wanted to do was make those Department of Roads men think twice about ruining our town's history," he explained. "I don't think great-great-great grandfather Jebediah or his fellow residents would have been disturbed too much by a few small explosions and a handful of gates clanking."

Annabelle, Adriana and Ralph climbed down the ladder and shut the attic trapdoor.

"Remember, not a word to anyone," he said, smiling.

The next morning, not even the sound of the toaster popping could make the twins jump. Life was back to normal, and they were determined that the mystery of the severed head, the bloody hand and the clanking gates would remain as firmly closed as the attic manhole.

Hidden behind the pages of the *Ingleford Crier*, the twins' father was happily grumbling about politicians, police officers, protesters and pretty much everyone else. Suddenly, a news story caught his eye.

"HA!" he declared. "'Department of Roads personnel are refusing to work in the old Ingleford cemetery and plans are being drawn up to move the proposed off-ramp half a kilometre northwards.'"

He dropped the paper and beamed at his family.

"That's good news," said Teresa, buttering a piece of toast. "A lot of residents will be pleased that the cemetery won't be disturbed."

Teresa looked up at her husband and a curious expression came into her eyes.

"What is that ghostly green stuff you have on your face, Ralph? I thought it was just my imagination, but you seemed to be glowing all night long."

"Really, dear?" replied Ralph innocently. He winked at the twins, and they smiled back.

A low, ghoulish, ghastly chuckling arose from three people seated around the table, and outside, a lone crow could be heard *craw-crawing* in the distance. Teresa's eyes flicked from person to person nervously. What had gotten into her family?

Adriana, Annabelle and Ralph knew they'd have to let Teresa into their cemetery secret sooner or later – but, like all good horror stories, the best part was keeping their unsuspecting victim in suspense for as long as possible.